At Matthew's Knee

A Poetic Commentary

on

the Gospel of Matthew

by

Kimberly Beyer-Nelson

Cover design by Kathy Haug
You can contact Kathy for cover design ideas at:
http://ferncreekassociates.com/

Acknowledgements

Special thanks to Cedars Unitarian
Universalist Church and
The Suquamish United Church of
Christ—
for giving me space to speak these
words aloud
as liturgy, as art and as individual
expression.

Thanks also to all the teachers of the
Comparative Religion Graduate
Program at Western Michigan
University, especially Dr. Francis
Gross. I hope I learned enough to keep
asking the tough questions.

Before we begin…a gentle prayer and reminder:

I who know, and do not know that I
know:
Let me be whole
Let me be awake.

I who have known, but do not know:
Let me once more see
The beginning of it all.

I who do not wish to know,
But still say that I wish to know:
Let me be guided
To safety and light.

I who do not know,
And know that I do not know:
Let me through this knowledge, know.

I who do not know, but think that I

know:

Set me free

From the confusion

Of that ignorance.

(Anonymous Islamic Prayer)

This is all I want to do –

put so much space between each letter

of the Word

that you must read the entire cosmos

to catch the meaning.

And in truth,

this is how it has always been.

KBN

Chapter 1

Matthew 1:1-17

The book of the genealogy of Jesus
Christ, the son of David, the son of
Abraham. Abraham became the father
of Isaac, Isaac the father of Jacob,
Jacob the father of Judah and his
brothers.
Judah became the father of Perez and
Zerah, whose mother was Tamar.
Perez became the father of Hezron,
Hezron the father of Ram,
Ram the father of Amminadab.
Amminadab became the father of
Nahshon, Nahshon the father of
Salmon,
Salmon the father of Boaz, whose
mother was Rahab. Boaz became the
father of Obed, whose mother was
Ruth. Obed became the father of Jesse,
Jesse the father of David the king.
David became the father of Solomon,
whose mother had been the wife of

Uriah.

*Solomon became the father of
Rehoboam, Rehoboam the father of
Abijah, Abijah the father of Asaph.
Asaph became the father of
Jehoshaphat, Jehoshaphat the father of
Joram, Joram the father of Uzziah.
Uzziah became the father of Jotham,
Jotham the father of Ahaz, Ahaz the
father of Hezekiah.
Hezekiah became the father of
Manasseh, Manasseh the father of
Amos, ⁴ Amos the father of Josiah.
Josiah became the father of Jechoniah
and his brothers at the time of the
Babylonian exile.*

*After the Babylonian exile, Jechoniah
became the father of Shealtiel,
Shealtiel the father of Zerubbabel,*

Zerubbabel the father of Abiud. Abiud became the father of Eliakim, Eliakim the father of Azor, Azor the father of Zadok. Zadok became the father of Achim, Achim the father of Eliud, Eliud the father of Eleazar. Eleazar became the father of Matthan, Matthan the father of Jacob,

Jacob the father of Joseph, the husband of Mary. Of her was born Jesus who is called the Messiah.

Thus the total number of generations from Abraham to David is fourteen generations; from David to the Babylonian exile, fourteen generations; from the Babylonian exile to the Messiah, fourteen generations.

Commentary

Three groups of fourteen generations,
but no faces.
The children, silent.
And the dog who thrust his nose into a
hand,
dust driven.
It is someone else's family tree,
a tribe of names.

What tears were cried?
What hand crafted their food?
How did cloth feel against their skin
when the wind ran hot and dry?
When they were ill, what lips bent
and brushed fevered brow?
And how did laughter sound,
echoing against
what
walls and
where?

I know the names link You to

the blood lines of kings,

to a people, a chain of time

but

where do these lineages run now?

I see a limited You in a list of names,

You,

the sight behind billions of eyes,

the very twist in our DNA,

near as, they say, the jugular vein.

Matthew 1:18

Now the birth of Jesus the Messiah took place in this way. When his mother Mary had been engaged to Joseph, but before they lived together, she was found to be with child from the Holy Spirit.

Commentary

The real birth happens within,
and of course,
she's virginal.

Aren't we all?

We look into each other's faces, and
see the spark,
the sperm, perhaps.
But the quickening,

but the birth,

Slides out within us,

sticky, warm, bursting with cries and

tight fists;

a bit of Spirit,

a bit of Mind

a bone of memory,

the subtle fanning veins of experience,

and then,

such a heartbeat!

Added like a Talking Drum

to our ever broadening circle.

Matthew 1:19

Her husband, Joseph, being a righteous man and unwilling to expose her to public disgrace, planned to dismiss her quietly.

Commentary

The woman in the check out lane,
flips the pages of the newest tabloid,
shaking her head and clucking.

An aisle over, a man scratches himself,
and
snuffs back snot with a hint of
satisfaction.

Behind me, a couple bickers about
corn flake brands,
and salt intake
and dairy farming practices,

while a teen named Angela,

fingers flying across the keypad

won't even look up.

She's tried before, I think,

to catch a smile, a gracious hello,

to share a secret eye to eye

over hamburger and broccoli.

But today,

she makes believe she is just part of

the machine.

I wonder if she, too, has awakened

something inside her,

so immense that she swells for

someone to see.

Perhaps, late at night, the man she

loves holds

his fingers to her lips,

Shhhhhhh.

He knows the people who run through

her lane

will not

understand.

Matthew 1:20

But just when he had resolved to do this, and angel of the Lord appeared to him in a dream and said, "Joseph, son of David, do not be afraid to take Mary as your wife, for the child conceived in her is of the Holy Spirit."

Commentary

Violin, play,
horsehair, and gut and wood,
Trinity of our own selves,
spirit, body and mind,
in kind
and discernment, each note
weaving and wedding,
until the angel nods in time as
wooden resolutions
evolve.

Matthew 1:21-23

She will bear a son and you are to name him Jesus, because he will save his people from their sins. All this took place to fulfill what the Lord had said through the prophet: "Behold, the virgin shall be with child and bear a son, and they shall name him Emmanuel," which means "God is with us."

Commentary

What parent has not,
resting hands on swelling belly,
searched to Name the faceless?

Here, the outward thrust of a tiny heel,
there the ripple beneath drum-taunt skin,
something hiccoughing in the Deep.

Do we not all whisper Emmanuel

in such a place?

Matthew 1: 24–25.

When Joseph awoke, he did as the
angel of the Lord had commanded him
and took his wife into his home. He
had no relations with her until she
bore a son, and he named him Jesus.

Commentary

Allow me to settle my shoes by the
door,
my toes curled against a threadbare
woolen rug,
pass the cup and bowl of thick soup,
light the candle above the mantel.

No, leave the TV off,
let the stereo grow silent
and listen instead to the rain
nodding the spring branches beyond
the window.

Draw the comforter up,
dog hair and all
and let your breath fall
on my scalp like prayer.

Oh, God,
name me home.

Chapter Two

Matthew 2: 1–2

After Jesus was born in Bethlehem in
Judea, during the time of King Herod,
Magi from the east came to Jerusalem
and asked, "Where is the one who has
been born king of the Jews? We saw
his star in the east and have come to
worship him."

I've marked a lot of books with stars,
printed carefully in the columns.
Neater than underlining, or rather,
less intrusive for the readers who
might come after.

Stars give me a lot of space to write
around and about,
my own yea and nays and
scribbled "wows".

Wahe Guru, the Sikh sing,
Wow! Teacher, light-bringer,

I'm open to hearing

You teach.

But emphasis on Wow!

Emphasis on preparing to hear

without needing to respond right

away.

This encompasses

the star I put

by the word

Worship.

Matthew 2:3-6

When King Herod heard this he was disturbed, and all Jerusalem with him. When he had called together all the people's chief priests and teachers of the law, he asked them where the Christ was to be born. In Bethlehem in Judea," they replied, "for this is what the prophet has written:

But you, Bethlehem, in the land of Judah,

are by no means least among the rulers of Judah;

for out of you will come a ruler

who will be the shepherd of my people Israel.'

Commentary

She rubs a little at her nose.

The trees are flowering again,

the first of the petals on the air already

wind–driven and fragrant.

The ferry blows mournful at the port,

the wild geese honk in return,

winter passing on a rainy wing.

She cradles her box of sidewalk chalk

against her belly,

and then presses blue to the gray

concrete.

Not much traffic here in the trailer

court.

And so the spring day passes,

arcs of color,

runny nose,

first daffodils bobbing in her mother's

curbside garden.

"Beautiful," someone says in passing,

bound for someplace important

no doubt.

A small cat lingers on the sidewalk,

watching the play of shadow and
pastel pink,
the sure movement of those small
human hands,
she who hasn't learned the laws of
pastel,
the boundary lines of copyright,
and the known fact that
God speaks only to
thinkers and leaders and academics
and officially recognized saints;
that God must be sifted through and
argued
crushed into words
that we might have
Meaning.

For a moment, she looks up,
cat eyes, human eyes,
meet,
And all of creation
Recites.

Matthew 2.7-8

*Then Herod called the Magi secretly
and found out from them the exact
time the star had appeared. He sent
them to Bethlehem and said, "Go and
make a careful search for the child. As
soon as you find him, report to me, so
that I too may go and worship him."*

Commentary

A wise minister said,
the long self-help bookshelf
is the saddest place in the world.

All those titles,
pointing up what you are not --
not pretty, not smart or desirable
not good at chess, a loser in art,
in short
a dummy.

We make other people rich

when they point out what we

are not.

And the saddest truth?

We're actually more comfortable

that way.

When a star is rising, brilliant,

something hurts our eyes.

We turn away,

and prefer the ground,

the blanket,

the TV and sofa.

We like our small sovereignty,

no matter if we are tyrant in 900

square feet,

keeping the counter clean,

laundry in perfect order,

work at 8 AM,

bed at 10.

But go to the window now!

Rip back the shade and behold,

what star is rising

above your own apartment?

And who else

will

see?

Matthew 2:9-12

After they had heard the king, they
went on their way, and the star they
had seen in the east went ahead of
them until it stopped over the place
where the child was. When they saw
the star, they were overjoyed. On
coming to the house, they saw the
child with his mother Mary, and they
bowed down and worshiped him.
Then they opened their treasures and
presented him with gifts of gold and of
incense and of myrrh. And having
been warned in a dream not to go
back to Herod, they returned to their
country by another route.

Commentary

They came with their gifts,
their starry eyes focused on a moment
in time,
then said their own kind of Namastes,
and departed on their own paths,
dream-driven and changed
undoubtedly
but still Magi.

Mary whispered, "I'm glad they came
and I'm glad they didn't stay."
She resolutely pushed the gifts away
and lay down exhausted
with eyes only for You.
You rested between your parents,
eyes closed now, lips pursed around
Mystery.

This is the sovereign wisdom of all
worship:

Dig a deep hole of faith,

But don't jump into it.

Matthew 2:13

*When they had gone, an angel of the
Lord appeared to Joseph in a dream.
"Get up," he said, "take the child and
his mother and escape to Egypt. Stay
there until I tell you, for Herod is
going to search for the child to kill
him."*

Commentary

Should you have cried out then,
Joseph?
Should you
have run through the villages,
yelling for the children to hide,
for mothers to secret themselves
their children
into the hills?

We have only the now in these words

poised between a birthing night

and the journey's first step.

The Mahabharata says,

"When any mother loves her own

child

more than any other,

there will be war."

The world has not really recognized

Herod,

Joseph,

staring so ferociously from our own

mirrors.

In the end,

run, fight or freeze,

we are really waiting, each of us,

for the angel.

Matthew 2:14-15

*So he [Joseph] got up, took the child
and his mother during the night and
left for Egypt, where he stayed until
the death of Herod. And so was
fulfilled what the Lord had said
through the prophet: "Out of Egypt I
called my son."*

Commentary

How I long for an Egypt,
a place to flee to,
a geography of tangibles.

I have searched for it
on windswept northern shores
in skyscrapers framed against
mountain sides
in silent naves
by gravestones

in marriage

on a sitting cushion,

before a loom

in the notes of a flute

on the back of a horse.

I still secretly wish for my mother and

father to take me there,

for an angel to speak and then

they would gather me up in the night

and flee to a geography

we cannot fathom alone.

There we would huddle, as a family,

waiting for Herod to die

within.

Matthew 2:16-18

When Herod realized that he had been
outwitted by the Magi, he was furious,
and he gave orders to kill all the boys
in Bethlehem and its vicinity who
were two years old and under, in
accordance with the time he had
learned from the Magi. Then what was
said through the prophet Jeremiah was
fulfilled:

"A voice is heard in Ramah,
weeping and great mourning,
Rachel weeping for her children
and refusing to be comforted,
because they are no more."

Commentary

At twenty, I had forty-year-old teeth,
ground them in my sleep
until my jaw popped and inflamed.

Some cries can't come out right away.

I wonder if some archeologist,
someone/where
hefted a warrior's skull,
probed stubby broken teeth,
and wondered about chewing leather
or tough nuts. Maybe
didn't hear the night-time wails
echoing around that dusty cavity.

I know a secret: Rachel had every one
of her
strong
ivory
teeth.

Matthew 2.19-20

After Herod died, an angel of the Lord

appeared in a dream to Joseph in

Egypt and said, "Get up, take the child

and his mother and go to the land of

Israel, for those who were trying to

take the child's life are dead."

Commentary

Those

other faces we don't see

behind the unjust laws,

the killing edict,

kitchen sink plumbers

working the disposal

legs sticking out

but no faces.

Not yet.

Maybe not ever.

Those

shadows,

behind thrones,

Oval Office seats,

and living room couches,

breathe.

Those Who Were

ever Are

and

Joseph will know

In his heart,

It is never

just

about

the obvious one:

the Herod,

the angel

or

some supposedly far away

God.

Matthew 2:21-23

So he got up, took the child and his mother and went to the land of Israel. But when he heard that Archelaus was reigning in Judea in place of his father Herod, he was afraid to go there. Having been warned in a dream, he withdrew to the district of Galilee, and he went and lived in a town called Nazareth. So was fulfilled what was said through the prophets: "He will be called a Nazarene."

Commentary

When we embrace the child,
we embrace the embryonic fluid.
With belly-breath we journey,
able to put toes in our mouth
stare at a point of light for minutes
sleep anywhere and when

Or not at all.

Breast beats warm,

Wet diaper 3 AM visions,

Muffled blanket music.

Four times you have dreamed, Joseph.

The child?

Always.

Chapter Three

Matthew 3:1-3

In those days John the Baptist came, preaching in the Desert of Judea and saying, "Repent, for the kingdom of heaven is near." This is he who was spoken of through the prophet Isaiah:

"A voice of one calling in the desert,
  'Prepare the way for the Lord,
  make straight paths for him.'

Commentary

Desert man,
Dusty man,
the kingdom is on your tongue
right now.

You can taste it in the furnace glare
smell it in the locust you eat

feel it the warped curve of the horizon.

Bring those of earth to water,

immersing

Birth them to air again,

and fire effortless devotion

in dripping chests.

Wipe open their eyes,

so they, too, call,

"Repent of these small selves"

And behold the face of God.

Matthew 3: 4-6

John's clothes were made of camel's

hair, and he had a leather belt around

his waist. His food was locusts and

wild honey. People went out to him

from Jerusalem and all Judea and the

whole region of the Jordan. Confessing

their sins, they were baptized by him

in the Jordan River.

Commentary

Take a bite,
a thin slice of memory.

Even dipped in honey,
some still pucker your lips.
Don't imagine that water
can age an unripe fruit,
or pressing it between
a few crumbs of bread will

not sour your stomach.

The locust stares down

from the tree,

unblinking

rubs a quick leg over his eye

polishing.

He has eaten ripe fruit.

He has also chewed the spring leaf,

leapt through the air,

defying gravity

for a time, the fullness of days

warm, simple and straightforward.

And so,

becoming part of John

(or even something vaster)

for him

is

no

great

tragedy.

Matthew 3:7-8

But when he saw many of the
Pharisees and Sadducees coming to
where he was baptizing, he said to
them: "You brood of vipers! Who
warned you to flee from the coming
wrath? Produce fruit in keeping with
repentance."

Commentary

John, John,
could you strip away their titles and
simply
see them?

Put aside your meaning making and
warnings for a time.

Don't you think some part of them
came to simply be *seen?*

No matter.

Put your hands on them anyway,

drop them back into the current

and let the water rush through them,

through this "you" holding them,

let the river play

over stones and through fish gills

leaping into droplets suspended in air.

Titles, names, roles swept away

if only for the space of one held

breath.

Then, midwife, hold them up

and out of the water naked, gasping

like newborns.

Watch them stumble up the bank

without a name or coin or certificate,

air and sunshine and tentative smiles

rippling through their watery selves.

Keep your ear to the river, John.

Titles and vipers and wrath and

baptisms

are shallow vessels

compared to where this water is

headed.

Matthew 3.9–10

*And do not think you can say to
yourselves, 'We have Abraham as our
father.' I tell you that out of these
stones God can raise up children for
Abraham. The ax is already at the root
of the trees, and every tree that does
not produce good fruit will be cut
down and thrown into the fire.*

Commentary

We know, with some part of our mind,
somewhere between
the novel character and
the raw birdsong before the light,
how deep our roots go.

Stone babies would still need breath,
still need the sun on their new faces

and a breast to comfort them

like warm soil.

Not all trees produce fruit you would

like, John.

Pine cones, thorns,

the ones of the long delicate leaf

fluttering shade all around them.

The smell of cedar,

the white paper dryness of the birch,

the tenacious mustard roots wrapping

through stony earth.

We would be

somehow

less

without them.

But here is the secret:

We all burn, John.

That's why we come to water.

Matthew 3:11-12

I baptize you with water for
repentance. But after me will come
one who is more powerful than I,
whose sandals I am not fit to carry. He
will baptize you with the Holy Spirit
and with fire. His winnowing fork is in
his hand, and he will clear his
threshing floor, gathering his wheat
into the barn and burning up the chaff
with unquenchable fire."

Commentary

Don't shout these words.
Whisper them, or better
sing them softly like a lullaby,
composed on a full harvest moon.

Unwrap yourself from your chaff,

surrender to the drying and the

settling

down with other grains.

Surrender to the mortar and pestle,

all of you, together at last.

Did you think only the chaff must

burn?

Let yourself be kneaded with water

with his hands,

with a bit of fat perhaps until

you are smooth, a little juicy, elastic.

And then cast yourself into the flame

to go dry again,

this, the rich lightness of spaciousness

that nourishes something larger.

You are here;

Spirit will begin casting grains

on uncertain ground,

and you will become

the harvest once more.

Matthew 3:15

Jesus replied, "Let it be so now; it is proper for us to do this to fulfill all righteousness." Then John consented.

Commentary

What does this water know of
Guru protocol?
It rushes by,
cold here in the shade of trees,
life in its belly,
snaking along the ground
and over stones stripped
of moss.
Bee and locust carried away,
dust, too,
and years.

John lives close to the water;
he knows when it leaps its banks

it pulls like human hands,

grasping,

plowing,

digging beneath roots,

submerging.

There will be fresh earth left behind,

rich and dark.

But first,

the roiling waters

erase boundaries,

rearrange landmarks,

smash the precarious structure

to its foundation.

He also knows

every so often

someone will dare to

ride that flood.

And when that one faces the swollen

river,

he or she will face it alone.

Matthew 3:16 –17

As soon as Jesus was baptized, he went up out of the water. At that moment heaven was opened, and he saw the Spirit of God descending like a dove and lighting on him. And a voice from heaven said, "This is my Son, whom I love; with him I am well pleased."

Commentary

One YES,
that's how it begins.

One kindly gaze,
one nod of approval,
one hug,
and the magical surfboard appears
the flood-rider,
the floater-on-the deep, rocking
in the swells.

Hug someone close and lo!

Look up at the beating wings,

white against the gray skies.

Chapter Four

Matthew 4:1

Then Jesus was led by the Spirit into
the desert to be tempted by the devil.

Commentary

Wake up, sleepwalker!
Lift your eyes from Facebook.
You are more than passive voice,
Even when led into your deserts.

Start small,
noticing
the lizard there, on the stone.
Or here,
the smallest dip in that branch
where a hummingbird could sit,
might sit.
Watch for her.

Then, maybe, notice the shadow,

breathing,

watching,

cast by each tiny grain of sand.

Hunger there, yes, and

hurts,

stone faces,

the resounding NOs of your life.

Dip your face close.

See the miniature boulders,

know their fissures and raw edges,

then watch it all

sift through your fingers.

The updraft of the dove's wings

will scatter it all in the wind.

Matthew 4:2

After fasting forty days and forty
nights, he was hungry.

Commentary

The desert:
where we bring our hunger with us.

It's not the same for each –
the craving behind the Coke;
behind the "A";
behind the Extreme Sport.

The gut wrench of
the sought-after smile,
the too-polite applause,
the oily sidelong glance.

It all nibbles at our gut
lifetimes snacking

on

ourselves.

And here,

we must at last come

out from the umbrella shade,

out from the gazebo

out from the fanning book.

The hot sun overhead,

cooking us

well done

indeed.

Matthew 4:3

The tempter came to him and said, "If you are the Son of God, tell these stones to become bread."

Commentary

We already know how to do that,
Tempter within.

We have eaten the strangest meals,
waved our hands over them and
called them Kosher or
nutritious
or good for us.
Chewed them until our teeth broke,
until our stomachs rebelled,
until the pancreas flopped
until our hearts
Stopped up, sodden.

Maybe all we really needed,

was a prayer of forgiveness and

thanksgiving intoned

over all those rocky places.

Matthew 4:4

Jesus answered, "It is written: 'Man does not live on bread alone, but on every word that comes from the mouth of God.'"

Commentary

Pull out your dictionary,
And then,
Having read,
Pull out every dictionary
Of every language,
And then
Having read,
Open your eyes to
The speech of the starry sky
Of water slipping down the river bed,
Of spring blossoms,
Of animal ear flicks and steady gazes

Of the wind's moan through your wild
hair.
Then,
Having read,
Open your mind to the memories,
The thoughts,
The imagination and intuition,
And then,
Having read
Go deeper into the silence
In the center of your own heart.

After all this,
You might catch a glimpse of one
Perfect Word
Coming from the mouth of God.

Matthew 4:5-6

Then the devil took him to the holy city and had him stand on the highest point of the temple. "If you are the Son of God," he said, "throw yourself down. For it is written:
" 'He will command his angels concerning you, and they will lift you up in their hands, so that you will not strike your foot against a stone."

Commentary

Trust Allah
and tie your camel...

We are beings of two real worlds,
intertwined,
One,
the heights that can kill,

the food that sustains,

the embrace of many arms,

the dull routine and

the flashing celebration.

The other,

the heights that can kill,

the food that sustains,

the embrace of many arms

the dull routine and

the flashing celebration.

Pull the words apart or

draw them in like breath.

Metaphor is still

Reality.

Matthew 4:7

Jesus answered him, "It is also written:
'Do not put the Lord your God to the
test.'

Commentary

Whether we fall or rise,

sleep in or race to the office,

craft the painting in slow

brushstrokes,

or gaze at the ultrasound machine and

needle

who do we test?

Who tests us?

If we step off the cliff,

or if we step back,

if we ride the flood,

or if we hunker by the river bank,

Do you not know?

Can you not feel it?

Take your Teacher's hand,
bring it to your lips.
There, in that perfect space between
skin and skin,
who are you?

Matthew 4:8-9

Again, the devil took him to a very high mountain and showed him all the kingdoms of the world and their splendor. "All this I will give you," he said, "if you will bow down and worship me."

Commentary

And you looked then,
eyes scanning from horizon to
horizon.
No lines of kingdoms,
no signs proclaiming principalities,
just sky and earth and
thin lines of people undulating their
way
to distant markets and funeral grounds
smoke curling from thousands of
hearths,
music and yelling and laughter

rippling from all those throats,

finally

a hawk cried shrill in the air

free of jesses and hood.

With each breath of air,

with each blink in the blistering light

you already know

how many times you will bow

and serve in the name of love,

exploring this wild sovereignty

of the servant.

Matthew 4:10

Jesus said to him, "Away from me,

Satan! For it is written: 'Worship the

Lord your God, and serve him only."

Commentary

Sometime I think,

evil is a tightness,

a too-narrow crack in the wall

letting in muddled light.

Or like consciousness

pressed into a small

corner of the back brain,

a space with only black and white,

and plugged directly

into flight or fight,

no other options:

free will twisted into

an imperative to act.

Then God must be

wide open eyes,

and a mind alive with fire

and light,

and yes, the heat of discipline that

holds a golden lamp high,

so even the deep black,

the labyrinth of shadows,

flares with brilliance

and

a profound,

alert

stillness.

Matthew 4:11

Then the devil left him, and angels

came and attended him.

Commentary

How small a shift it takes,

like dropping your gaze away from the

TV screen

and into the eyes of your child.

For a moment,

the wonder hits,

and then a new commercial kicks in.

Our minds flicker,

faster than computer screens,

so many computations

before bioelectricity becomes

thought

becomes

action

becomes

Ideology.

The problem has always been

how to

attend

like

angels.

Matthew 4:12-16

When Jesus heard that John had been

put in prison, he returned to Galilee.

Leaving Nazareth, he went and lived

in Capernaum, which was by the lake

in the area of Zebulun and Naphtali—

to fulfill what was said through the

prophet Isaiah:

"Land of Zebulun and land of Naphtali,

the way to the sea, along the Jordan,

Galilee of the Gentiles—

the people living in darkness

have seen a great light;

on those living in the land of the

shadow of death

a light has dawned."

Commentary

This time,

you went to water when you ached,

instead of the open stretch of desert.

This time, you preferred the wave,

the deep

the undulating ambiguity of water.

So much surface,

as far as the eye can see,

reflecting the moonlight

tracing patterns that do not hold.

Here, a prison bar,

there, a child's face,

John's voice on the beach,

calling you like a siren.

Wade out

Flood Rider

and allow the water

to lift you up

as it once did.

Then watch for the dove

to guide you to the shore.

Matthew 4:17

*From that time on Jesus began to
preach, "Repent, for the kingdom of
heaven is near."*

Commentary

I'm sorry,
for I did not look closely at
the tree that shaded my room
on smoldering summer days.

I did not notice
my brother's sadness
and the way
beer rocked him to sleep.

I did not look
into the eyes of the street person,
read his sign to closely,

or wonder if he was cold.

I'm sorry
that I am often more afraid
Of life than
death.

That I feel I can
read and know all about You
and teach those unchanging
Words with any authority.

That I heard music
and did not dance,
That I heard laughter
and did not join in,
That I watched my child play
and then, went back to my computer.

For all this and more,
I repent.

Matthew 4:18 and 19

As Jesus was walking beside the Sea of Galilee, he saw two brothers, Simon called Peter and his brother Andrew. They were casting a net into the lake, for they were fishermen. "Come, follow me," Jesus said, "and I will make you fishers of men."

Commentary

Petros
A Rock afloat;
Did you smile when you saw them,
understand somehow that paradox
would be the boat for your words?

Oh, but you didn't tell them:
what they catch,
they are responsible for.

At least, you kept that secret for a bit.

Fish are easy;
scales become skin,
flat eyes learn to blink
And sometimes
they return to the water
riding the waves and laughing.

People, though,
are harder to pull inside.
They shift under the skin
and upend the mind-boat
and find ways
to cut through the net,
and flop their way
Back toward the land.

Matthew 4:20

At once they left their nets and

followed him.

Commentary

What good a net?
when the flood has come ashore,
and the very land underfoot
slips.
The water so muddy that fish
hunker and gasp in the
thick of it all.

Even a boat
Could not ride the waves
that thundered like surf in that voice.
They had to throw themselves in,
strike out, arm over arm,
hungry
to see the face of the man
standing firm in the waves.

And having seen,

nothing to do but follow.

Matthew 4:21-22

Going on from there, he saw two other brothers, James son of Zebedee and his brother John. They were in a boat with their father Zebedee, preparing their nets. Jesus called them, and immediately they left the boat and their father and followed him.

Commentary

How my old hands tremble
as I mend the nets tonight.
The fire light is not enough to work by,
not anymore.

See, here is the finger that the big fish
took,;
And there,
the scar from gutting another.

Fish cuts rot the flesh;

I consider myself lucky--

I still have my hands.

My wife,

she lay herself down on the beach five

years ago,

and sighed her breath into the waves.

And now, this simple little rest I take,

sitting in the darker shadow of my

boat,

gives me too much time to wonder,

to grit my teeth,

and feel tears in the gray of my beard.

Just what was it James and John saw

in that strange and quiet man?

And why wasn't I

Enough?

Matthew 4:23

Jesus went throughout Galilee,

teaching in their synagogues,

preaching the good news of the

kingdom, and healing every disease

and sickness among the people.

Commentary

Teacher,

What questions did they ask?

Or did they sit

and whisper among themselves

while their eyes stayed on your face,

looking for more fleshy answers.

Preacher,

did they wonder how one

dusty from the road,

with wet and kind eyes,

could say anything that mattered,

they, who would fold the bread-

dough,

pour the new wine in wooden cups,

on only some lucky days?

Healer,

did you take their gratitude

as your only payment,

and find even that

Chafed like rope

around your own neck?

How much did you point beyond

yourself

to the calm upholding the restless

waves,

and why did they see

only

your

broken

nails?

Matthew 4:24

News about him spread all over Syria,

and people brought to him all who

were ill with various diseases, those

suffering severe pain, the demon-

possessed, those having seizures, and

the paralyzed, and he healed them.

Commentary

I watched a man on the park bench,
his head bowed almost to his lap,
his shoulders shaking.
A boy threw a rock at a gull,
and laughed when it hit true
followed by a wet and garbled squawk.
A purebred dog, excited by it all,
fell slathering to the pavement,
his owner, holding the leash,
blushed red with embarrassment
and sank down beside him.

I stood paralyzed,

waiting

for

the healing

to

wash over us all.

I would have run to one who had

any

Answer.

Matthew 4.25

Large crowds from Galilee, the

Decapolis, Jerusalem, Judea and the

region across the Jordan followed him.

Commentary

Most of us,

we would not do this now,

leave the computer and office

and follow a teacher as he wandered.

Or maybe we would,

and take pictures with our cell phones

and Twitter to our friends.

But would we see, would we hear,

bend knees and sit on cement,

shade our heads with our I-Pads,

and try to peer inside his words?

Did those ancient crowds do any
better?
Schooling like fish, kicking up a froth
of dust.
Perhaps they at least sensed
it is important to seek
Beyond
even if you aren't quite sure what you
are really looking for.

Chapter 5

Matthew 5:1

Now when he saw the crowds, he went up on a mountainside and sat down. His disciples came to him...

Commentary

The crowds ebbed away,
fading down the shoulders of the hill
as you climbed.

It felt good to stretch,
to dig into dry earth
and simply breathe.

Then you took your seat.

You watched your fishermen
hunker in the light,
their eyes still dazed,

their clothing skewed

finger twitching,

jostled within,

seeking land legs.

And so you waited a bit,

feeling the earth holding you up

and the sky like a vast ocean overhead

impenetrable blue,

and considered

the vast distance between

word

and

presence.

Matthew 5:2-3

…and he began to teach them saying:

"Blessed are the poor in spirit, for

theirs is the kingdom of heaven.

Commentary

He snatched the credit card out of the

other man's hand,

and ripped it through the card reader

before flinging it

back in his general direction.

His black hair swung around his

shoulders,

the row of silver earrings hoops

tinkling against each other as he

moved,

his eyes set fierce on the register

screen.

And the customer

drew in a soft breath,

said his Word down deep into his

belly--

the word that pointed to

stillness,

presence

awareness,

softened his face,

dropped his shoulders

and when the clerk turned back,

human eye met human eye--

what happened then?

Matthew 5:5

Blessed are the meek, for they will

inherit the earth.

Commentary

Sun is

Green leaf,

Desert sand

Is water

Sluicing rock,

Black pressure,

Is wind

Rippling grass,

Shattering trees,

Is earth,

Thrust of mountain

Spiral of cave,

Is heart--

How can we be anything but meek

In the face of such an inheritance?

Matthew 5:6

*Blessed are those who hunger and
thirst for righteousness, for they will
be filled.*

Commentary

I want to be more than a
stone Buddha;
Let me be malleable wood, like
the statue thrown in the fire
when the zendo shuddered in the
cold--
then the monks could feel me right to
their bones.

I want to be more than the cursive
flair,
my name set in precious gemstones
and gold,
Rather,

fan someone with the Book

until the sweat dries on their face,

and they breathe in deep.

I want to be more than a pendant,

swinging from a groovy hemp strand,

bouncing in time with shopping steps,

Rather,

I want someone to moan me out,

in the dark,

afraid no one will hear.

Matthew 5:7

Blessed are the merciful, for they will be shown mercy.

Commentary

Wipe her nose, help with his
homework, forgive and forgive, listen
to her story again (and again), take
chocolate chip cookies to D&D, plant a
tree, bake bread with your own hands,
hear the cat cry in the night, think
about emails carefully, never go to bed
angry, drive the speed limit, wave
someone ahead of you in line, put your
legs up the wall and rest, send a letter
to the editor, lift weights, fold each
shirt with the prayer, send a birthday
card, feed the birds in your backyard,
repaint the teen center, smile at the
grocery clerk, use the library, walk

with your neighbor, throw a potluck,
color with crayons, enjoy used clothes,
keep your car for more than three
years, shop the farmer's market, pet a
critter, throw open your window to
the cold, stop on a sidewalk for no
reason, call your mom, eat fudge and
popcorn while watching Avatar, scrub
off a stop sign, thank your teachers...

Come now!
Even thirty gig can't contain all this!
You'll need to keep going--

Matthew 5:8

Blessed are the pure in heart, for they will see God.

Commentary

They walked to the corner store,

A mom and her eight year old,

Flip-flops slapping the pavement,

holding hands where the highway ran

fast

And curved.

Never enough money to make all the

bills

but today was payday

and that meant ice cream --

one scoop of Blue Moon on a sugar

cone.

And coming home,

the geese flew high

against blue-gray clouds,

voices ringing.

And low, just topping the hill,

a rainbow

just before the rain began

again.

Matthew 5:9

*Blessed are the peacemakers, for they
will be called sons of God.*

Commentary

His face, her face,

hat word

This insult,

Not enough

Too much

Why did she do that?

Why don't I care?

When will I die?

Not another shower

Another dinner

Another laundry load.

I miss Grandpa,

Lighten up, brother.

Too much salt,

Not enough exercise,

Money, money, money.

Religion is a lie,

And the cartoonist got it right

After all.

And joy is what we are

at the core.

The Yes, Our YES!

Hello daughter, hello son.

Matthew 5:10

*Blessed are those who are persecuted
because of righteousness, for theirs is
the kingdom of heaven.*

Commentary

The day after the twin towers fell,
9/12, nothing remarkable,
He stood up in class,
only a seventh grader,
skinny, acne,
and looked his social studies teacher in
the eye.

"What did you say?" the teacher
demanded again.

The boy squared his jaw,
locked his gaze on the adult.

"What was OUR part in this?" he said again.

No apologies in that slender frame.

The teacher pointed a shaking finger to the door.

"Get out!"

Sometimes right is
defiant,
dangerous,
foolish
and
gives you a day off school.

Matthew 5:11-12

Blessed are you when people insult
you, persecute you and falsely say all
kinds of evil against you because of
me. Rejoice and be glad, because great
is your reward in heaven, for in the
same way they persecuted the
prophets who were before you.

Commentary

I remember an old teaching story –

A man sat alone in a cave in the
Himalayas
perfect in his peace,
gentle, kind, full of equanimity.

When he felt the time had come to
teach,
he deported himself with dignity

down to the market place –

where the children made fun of him,

and the smells of the donkeys,

monkeys and cows

assaulted him,

movement and color blinded him,

then,

finally,

an ox cart splashed him

head to foot with mud.

He threw down his staff and yelled at

everything

until red in the face.

We're often like that foolish man

When really

we are

surrounded by

true prophets.

Matthew 5:13

You are the salt of the earth. But if the salt loses its saltiness, how can it be made salty again? It is no longer good for anything, except to be thrown out and trampled by men.

Commentary

He held up one shaking thumb,

his neck and throat too burned from

the radiation

to utter "last one."

I'm not sure anyone heard him ring

the bell--

that celebration that peels out

when treatment is finally done.

Such a small ritual, really,

an entry way into the long hall of

survival.

The docs wanted him to stay at
hospital;
oxygen levels failing, sores weeping,
but he waved them off with his
baseball cap,
hunched into his flannel shirt, head
shaking.
Everything about him said,
"last one."

He sketched a smile for me,
then,
big-knuckled hands limp between his
knees,
he let himself be pushed into the
sunlight
and out to the shining white car
waiting for him.
His driver read the last lines of her
book
before getting out and helping him in,
all six foot two of him,

Ashen faced,

breathing tube,

and two women mid-wifing his last

trip for treatment.

Salt on his lips.

Salt on the cold winter pavement.

Salt in my eyes.

Matthew 5:14-16

You are the light of the world. A city on a hill cannot be hidden. Neither do people light a lamp and put it under a bowl. Instead they put it on its stand, and it gives light to everyone in the house. In the same way, let your light shine before men, that they may see your good deeds and praise your Father in heaven.

Commentary

Golden spire,
perfect stillness,
purple to blue to orange to white,
gradations fixed like rainbow stripes,
no perfumes or special colors,
not even bees wax
to feed the flame.

Hand cupped by hand,

eyes cast down

seeing everything and nothing.

Left leg falling asleep,

Mind wanders, comes back, like

breath.

Old sweatpants,

sock with a small hole starting,

bits of yarn on the floor,

dust on Buddha and Om and the

Cross.

And then

"Time for school, Ian."

Cereal bowl, clashing silverware,

the grumbling child,

the dishwasher not run last night,

dog spins by the door, wanting out,

rain lashes the window in a sudden

gust.

Golden spire,

perfect stillness

no perfumes or special colors,

not even bees wax

to feed the flames--

even when nobody notices.

Matthew 5:17-20

Do not think that I have come to abolish the Law or the Prophets; I have not come to abolish them but to fulfill them. I tell you the truth, until heaven and earth disappear, not the smallest letter, not the least stroke of a pen, will by any means disappear from the Law until everything is accomplished. Anyone who breaks one of the least of these commandments and teaches others to do the same will be called least in the kingdom of heaven, but whoever practices and teaches these commands will be called great in the kingdom of heaven. For I tell you that unless your righteousness surpasses that of the Pharisees and the teachers of the law, you will certainly not enter the kingdom of heaven.

Commentary

Pay attention.

Pay attention now.

I heard the car hit the van,

right there, in the snowy intersection.

breath-taking how metal can shriek,

how glass, in flight, hangs for a

moment like

snowflakes.

I stopped pumping gas and ran out

onto the road.

And the woman, gray hair frizzling,

already babbling, "my fault, I saw it

was red

but didn't stop,

daughter in the hospital all night,

I sat beside her; it's bad,

and now my coffee is soaking into my

white coat.

Where are my keys?"

Pay attention.

Pay attention now.

Like a pond ripple,

the ambulance, the police car

onlookers, gas station attendants,

passengers, other drivers,

myself and a stray dog,

coffee, not much blood,

stop light cycling on, un-minding,

all lapping at the edges of a simple

law:

Stop on red.

Pay attention.

Pay attention now.

The rest is pretty simple.

Matthew 5.21-22

You have heard that it was said to the people long ago, 'Do not murder, and anyone who murders will be subject to judgment.' But I tell you that anyone who is angry with his brother will be subject to judgment. Again, anyone who says to his brother, 'Raca', is answerable to the Sanhedrin. But anyone who says, 'You fool!' will be in danger of the fire of hell.

Commentary

We burn, sometimes
in the deep watches of the night,
when memory is cinematic
and the covers, like armor.
We pull out word weapons,
re-play the good fight,
over and over, until

if we are lucky,

spots of light appear in the film

of mind

and it all burns up and unravels into a

more sane sleep.

Matthew 5:23-24

*"Therefore, if you are offering your gift
at the altar and there remember that
your brother has something against
you, leave your gift there in front of
the altar. First go and be reconciled to
your brother; then come and offer
your gift."*

Commentary

Relational God,
who breathes in each form,
animate, inanimate,
sentient or spread across the sky as
volcanic dust,
any part of the heart held back
is a portion held back from you.

We dance a circle of light,
we dance a circle of dark,

weaving to your tabla and Vina.

Some of us, most of us,

aren't particularly graceful

in the rhythm of it all.

But here is a secret:

I cannot offer this rose to you,

without offering it to my brother.

Cannot pour out this wine

nor break this bread,

without it being the blood and bone

of all.

Each time I reconcile with my sister,

my brother,

I reconcile with you.

And honestly?

That's why Hallmark makes a killing.

Matthew 5:25–26

Settle matters quickly with your
adversary who is taking you to court.
Do it while you are still with him on
the way, or he may hand you over to
the judge, and the judge may hand you
over to the officer, and you may be
thrown into prison. I tell you the truth,
you will not get out until you have
paid the last penny.

Commentary

Sleep does not come,
and the prison of wakefulness,
presses in the dark.
We know the magic words of freedom,
Sorry.
My fault.
Let me take

the blame here.

But something stops us short,
and in the morning,
coffee is never enough.

Matthew 5:27-28

You have heard that it was said, 'Do not commit adultery. But I tell you that anyone who looks at a woman lustfully has already committed adultery with her in his heart.

Commentary

She stares at him across the lip of her
wine glass,
but he, distracted, fiddles with his
pasta.
Eye to eye, they might have seen,
might have shaken off
the way he lingered with his
coworker,
the other woman, soft spoken and
elegant.

Married of course, all of them.

The wine is too sweet,

she drops here eyes into

silence.

In that missed moment,

the very relationship of adultery.

Matthew 5:29-30

If your right eye causes you to sin,
gouge it out and throw it away. It is
better for you to lose one part of your
body than for your whole body to be
thrown into hell. And if your right
hand causes you to sin, cut it off and
throw it away. It is better for you to
lose one part of your body than for
your whole body to go into hell.

Commentary

The strawberry perches on the
counter,
fist-large, little green leaves
curling at its brow.
A spider creeps about the base,
reaches up with one tender leg,
touches,
then goes on its way.

He glances at the fruit for a moment,

just one thing among cups

and spilled sugar

and coffee steam

then deftly hefts and slices out the

unripe bits with his delicate steel knife.

Here's the secret of sin:

Perhaps if he watched more carefully

no knife

would

have

been

Necessary.

Matthew 5:31–32

It has been said, 'Anyone who divorces

his wife must give her a certificate of

divorce.' But I tell you that anyone

who divorces his wife, except for

marital unfaithfulness, causes her to

become an adulteress, and anyone

who marries the divorced woman

commits adultery.'

Commentary

I know you're a modern reader;
Don't recoil so fast.

I know you mind-paint the
abused woman,
whether she wears bruises within or
without
or

the "fathered" woman,

not allowed to grow up and out.

The changed man, no longer drinking

like his partner,

or the one who suffers in the silent

way,

tongue lashed and

empty at night.

How does marriage serve these souls?

Certificates don't bind wounds and

aloneness does not heal mistakes.

If all is change, except for the love of

God,

Why, then, this verse?

Let me ask you this:

What does divorce

or marriage for that matter

Really Mean?

Matthew 5: 33-37

"Again, you have heard that it was said to the people long ago, 'Do not break your oath, but keep the oaths you have made to the Lord.' But I tell you, Do not swear at all: either by heaven, for it is God's throne; or by the earth, for it is his footstool; or by Jerusalem, for it is the city of the Great King. And do not swear by your head, for you cannot make even one hair white or black. Simply let your 'Yes' be 'Yes,' and your 'No,' 'No'; anything beyond this comes from the evil one."

Commentary

He steps to the table,
eyes slightly downcast
but wholly present.
Ink stone

massages

water

massages

bowl,

and then,

the brush tip swirls just so,

lifts,

and

in a single sweep,

decisive,

direct

an ink circle blooms on the rice paper

just

like

it

Promised.

Matthew 5:38–42

"You have heard that it was said, 'Eye for eye, and tooth for tooth.' But I tell you, Do not resist an evil person. If someone strikes you on the right cheek, turn to him the other also. And if someone wants to sue you and take your tunic, let him have your cloak as well. If someone forces you to go one mile, go with him two miles. Give to the one who asks you, and do not turn away from the one who wants to borrow from you.

Commentary

Who are you?

If each woman is born
already carrying the eggs,
one vital half of her children,

waiting

for the other piece of themselves that

squirm about only for a day or three

before they grow still and cold,

eternity and the ephemeral meeting,

Who are you?

If our cells turn over

every seven years or so,

we are

essentially

Reborn.

So Who are you?

If once you were a child,

now bowed over the computer,

now sipping those last drops of water,

Who are You?

Who are you, *really?*

And who is the one who forces, strikes
or sues?

The qigong master knows
The world can only push
what is
already
Hardened.

Matthew 5: 43–48

You have heard that it was said, 'Love your neighbor and hate your enemy.' But I tell you: Love your enemies and pray for those who persecute you, that you may be sons of your Father in heaven. He causes his sun to rise on the evil and the good, and sends rain on the righteous and the unrighteous. If you love those who love you, what reward will you get? Are not even the tax collectors doing that? And if you greet only your brothers, what are you doing more than others? Do not even pagans do that? Be perfect, therefore, as your heavenly Father is perfect.

Commentary

Get beyond a sense of reward,
get beyond self and other,

right and left,

Mother and stranger,

enemy and lover.

I would have weeping, instead,

real tears as you pluck a flower

and watch how, in an afternoon,

It fades there on your kitchen counter.

We are not so very different.

I would have joyous dance,

wide flung arms, gaze upward

spinning, spinning,

until the earth calls us to sleep.

We are not so very different.

I would have eyes meeting eyes,

darkness pressing

bodies embracing in the night,

then to sweet sleep.

We are not so very different.

"Perfection" is to lose

Even

This

Word.

Chapter 6

Matthew 6:1-4

*"Be careful not to do your 'acts of
righteousness' before men, to be seen
by them. If you do, you will have no
reward from your Father in heaven.
"So when you give to the needy, do not
announce it with trumpets, as the
hypocrites do in the synagogues and
on the streets, to be honored by men. I
tell you the truth, they have received
their reward in full. But when you give
to the needy, do not let your left hand
know what your right hand is doing,
so that your giving may be in secret.
Then your Father, who sees what is
done in secret, will reward you."*

Commentary

FAH!
All this talk of reward
as if we were children

opening up our hand for a nickel.

Unless that reward is the very face of
God,
I want none of it.

Unless that reward is a loosening of
these
wants
and shoulds
and might have beens,
it is all still bondage.

As long as even one hand even
KNOWS
it does kindness, does righteousness,
labels it as something necessary,
something expected,
even
a way to seek reward from God in a
crafted silence,
It is already a chipped and broken

thing.

Matthew 6:5-8

"And when you pray, do not be like the hypocrites, for they love to pray standing in the synagogues and on the street corners to be seen by men. I tell you the truth, they have received their reward in full. But when you pray, go into your room, close the door and pray to your Father, who is unseen. Then your Father, who sees what is done in secret, will reward you. And when you pray, do not keep on babbling like pagans, for they think they will be heard because of their many words. Do not be like them, for your Father knows what you need before you ask him."

Commentary

I try to imagine,

only a begging bowl,

a walking stick,

simple hand-woven wrap around

a body more light and bone than

anything else.

I would gaze out on

the Ganges

undulating

carrying its little bowls of

human ash along to the sea,

past women washing their clothes,

and a Brahman finishing his morning

prayers.

The shelter slats the sunlight,

moves with the hours,

and only the folded hands

Namaste

as others pass.

Silence.

And in the night,

the insects buzzing,

yes, and even biting,

but the stars tip each ripple of the

river in light,

as I retire to the Guha,

the cave of the heart,

and listen for the still, small voice of

God.

Matthew 6:9-13

"This, then, is how you should pray:

" 'Our Father in heaven,

hallowed be your name,

your kingdom come,

your will be done

on earth as it is in heaven.

Give us today our daily bread.

Forgive us our debts,

as we also have forgiven our debtors.

And lead us not into temptation,

but deliver us from the evil one.'"

Commentary

Do you know another language?
Good!
Then speak the Lord's Prayer in that
one,
but only if it lets you hear the words
again.

Or even better, sing it,
so your breath runs round and full,
and vibrates in your nose,
in your chest.

Or throw open your arms and hands,
and sign it to the trees and your dog
and the old, old mirror over your
Chest of drawers.

Shake the words out, one by one,
write them,
cry them,
paint them out in brilliant and somber
colors,
plant them in your garden
knead them into your bread.

Without *you*,
these are just words.

Matthew 6:14-15

For if you forgive men when they sin
against you, your heavenly Father will
also forgive you. But if you do not
forgive men their sins, your Father will
not forgive your sins.

Commentary

Make me transparent, Lord,
or a reed, easily bending in the wind.
Nothing in the way,
nothing hard and unyielding to break,
flowing around wound and joy alike,
remembering the amoeba past,
the salty water self,
who not so much holds as upholds.
Let me cast my thoughts out as far as
they can reach,
into the dark places without stars,
pregnant places,

forgiving places,

full of space,

full of potential fire,

sacrificial fires

that bring the rain to ripen all things.

Matthew 6: 16–18

"When you fast, do not look somber as the hypocrites do, for they disfigure their faces to show men they are fasting. I tell you the truth, they have received their reward in full. But when you fast, put oil on your head and wash your face, so that it will not be obvious to men that you are fasting, but only to your Father, who is unseen; and your Father, who sees what is done in secret, will reward you.

Commentary

Runners

Vegans

Republican and Democrat,

Priest

Pew warmer

Doctor

Bagger

Dressage rider

Poet

Weight lifter

Quilter

Gamer

Musician

Soccer mom

Micro-loaner

All of them

and all of me

or you.

How public we make

our little fasts,

laying them out,

lifting a card, considering,

watching those around us carefully,

wondering if our personal stock has

risen.

She seems to sit a little more forward,

his eyes seem interested,

this gesture will ensure the money will

flow,

that glancing away

hopes

that she will move closer,

so he can show her just how hungry

he really is.

"We have a right to our actions,

But not the fruit thereof,"

said God to a warrior five hundred

year before

his verse was even

set to ink.

The greatest fast is from

The card game, the stock option,

The ongoing commerce

Of ourselves.

Matthew 6:19-21

*"Do not store up for yourselves
treasures on earth, where moth and
rust destroy, and where thieves break
in and steal. But store up for
yourselves treasures in heaven, where
moth and rust do not destroy, and
where thieves do not break in and
steal. For where your treasure is, there
your heart will be also.*

Commentary

Buddha has a word for this:
attachment
Then he asks of us a deeper question:
why do we attach?
What deep part of our mind grasps
not just jewelry or the show horse,
but the compelling idea,
the rousing emotion

the importance of this self?

If I hold the idea too tightly,
it creates a prison around me.

If I hold the emotion to highly,
even a sense like love,
it turns inward rather than out
stale bread, vinegar rather than wine.

And myself?
We are meant to be in motion,
in process,
in relationship.
The dance IS
where heaven and heart
whirl.

Matthew 6:19-21

*"Do not store up for yourselves
treasures on earth, where moth and
rust destroy, and where thieves break
in and steal. But store up for
yourselves treasures in heaven, where
moth and rust do not destroy, and
where thieves do not break in and
steal. For where your treasure is, there
your heart will be also.*

Commentary

I was asked
in front of my supervisors,
"What gets you out of bed in the
morning,
What brightens your step
Gives you energy?"

And for a while

I ran through all the right things to
say:
I love children
I love the church
I love organizing
and planning
and envisioning
the future.

But instead,
I spoke of the soft ply of heather yarns,
the feel of the pen in my hands as I
write,
holding my son in my arms
the deep quiet of meditation,
the exuberance of a yoga pose.

The supervisor shook her head,
Said it didn't sound like I even wanted
to be here.

Of course, she was speaking about

treasures on earth:

Saying the right things,

doing the interview just so,

making everyone comfortable.

But I have learned to base my life on

hardier stuff

Like creativity,

hugs and

still,

small

voices.

Matthew 6, 22-23

*"The eye is the lamp of the body. If
your eyes are good, your whole body
will be full of light. But if your eyes are
bad, your whole body will be full of
darkness. If then the light within you
is darkness, how great is that
darkness!*

Commentary

How quickly the dog looks away
his yawn covering
what his darting eyes cannot.

She continues to stare, but her mind
drifts, clouded, repetitive
or sometimes,
merely vastly tired.

While across the town,

he counts the scraps of paper on the
ground
his feet slapping pavement
his wallet like an anchor
as he steps by the homeless.

How often we cover our eyes
draw within,
lest we challenge the status quo
and
become
Light Bringers.

Matthew 6:24

"No one can serve two masters. Either he will hate the one and love the other, or he will be devoted to the one and despise the other. You cannot serve both God and Money."

Commentary

She crept in, really,
and found the very corner seat,
the very back seat
the very hidden seat.
She prayed small.
The sanctuary, darkened except for
dim winter light through stained glass
windows,
creaked like the ribcage of an ancient
beast.

The congregation had brought the

altar stones
all the way from Italy,
the parquet floors, from some closer
source.
Dark, oiled woods on the walls, and
red velvet on the chairs,

How great is God.

But only she could give him legs
and kindly eyes and a hand that could
reach down and pull another into the
life-raft with a simple "let me help."

And she prayed simple
And she prayed small,
Knowing the master she served,
Less tangible
More enduring.

Matthew 6: 25-27

"Therefore I tell you, do not worry about your life, what you will eat or drink; or about your body, what you will wear. Is not life more important than food, and the body more important than clothes? Look at the birds of the air; they do not sow or reap or store away in barns, and yet your heavenly Father feeds them. Are you not much more valuable than they? Who of you by worrying can add a single hour to his life?

Commentary

Lay yourself on the damp earth,
arms away from your sides, palms
turned to the sky
and breathe into your heart.

Can you feel the ground support you,

conform to leg and buttock,

asking you to spread out from sinew

and bone

to know what the rocks know--

the art of being held.

And above you,

the clouds tumbling past one another

light from millions of miles away

catching this leaf,

this squirrel tail

this upturned face.

Each exhale,

the earth.

Each inhale,

the heavens.

And the heart mediating,

Like the horizon between waking and

sleep,

like the hug before the school bus

like this moment

like this moment

like this moment.

Eternally.

Matthew 6.28–34

"And why do you worry about clothes?
See how the lilies of the field grow.
They do not labor or spin. Yet I tell you
that not even Solomon in all his
splendor was dressed like one of these.
If that is how God clothes the grass of
the field, which is here today and
tomorrow is thrown into the fire, will
he not much more clothe you, O you
of little faith? So do not worry, saying,
'What shall we eat?' or 'What shall we
drink?' or 'What shall we wear?' For
the pagans run after all these things,
and your heavenly Father knows that
you need them. But seek first his
kingdom and his righteousness, and all
these things will be given to you as
well. Therefore do not worry about
tomorrow, for tomorrow will worry
about itself. Each day has enough
trouble of its own."

Commentary

She drove a perfect blue Porche,

parked it next to muddy pickup trucks

and

cars yearning for an empty field,

aching for the season of falling apart.

She read Emerson and Thoreau to her

English lit classes,

cultured voice,

perfect nails, painted to match her

lipstick.

I considered her for half a year,

trying to make Porche and fingernails

rhyme with the snowy campus

with the boy who never wore his

underwear

under his loose sweats,

with all the coughs and sniffles born

of too-hot dorm rooms.

And in the end, I did ask her--
Why do you still need to teach?

And she laughed, her dark eyes
intense.
"Because otherwise, I would worry
about cornflakes...what brand,
how much for breakfast?
Do we have enough?
I'm going to worry...
I just want what I worry about
to
mean
something."

About the Author

Kimberly Beyer-Nelson holds a master's degree in comparative religion and loves teaching yoga, qigong and adult education classes when she is not writing, crafting fiber art or running after the sheep in her backyard. "My grandfather once said he was a jack of all trades and master of none. I think I have managed to live into that same sentiment my whole life, and I can't say it has ever disappointed me." Kim has authored three non-fiction titles and five science fiction works and her poetry has appeared in both national anthologies and national magazines.

Made in the USA
Charleston, SC
04 August 2014